Lighting

HOUSE & GARDEN

GUIDE TO EFFICIENCY AND GOOD LOOKS

by Leonie Highton

COLLINS – GLASGOW AND LONDON
IN ASSOCIATION WITH THE CONDÉ NAST PUBLICATIONS LTD

First published 1975
Published by WILLIAM COLLINS SONS AND COMPANY LIMITED
GLASGOW AND LONDON
in association with THE CONDÉ NAST PUBLICATIONS LIMITED
COPYRIGHT © 1975 THE CONDÉ NAST PUBLICATIONS LIMITED

Editorial services Youé and Spooner Limited

Printed in Great Britain
ISBN 0 00 435049 9

Contents

Acknowledgements: The following photographers are represented: Anghinelli, Jacques Bachmann, Aldo Ballo, Guido Bini, Jacques Boucher, Michael Boys, Emmett Bright, Derek Butler, Martin Chaffer, Giorgio Colombo, Horst D'Acourt, Attilio Delcomune, Jacques Dirand, Alain Dovifat, Richard Einzig, Leonardo Ferrante, Peter Fisher, Cristina Ghergo, Marianne Haas, David Hirsch, Joël Lelièvre, Kit Lepage, Gerard Martinet, David Massey, William Maywald, André Morain, James Mortimer, Jay A. Myrdal, Michael Nicholson, Spike Powell, Primois/Pinto, Henk Snoek, Ezra Stoller, Tim Street-Porter, Alain Spy, Colin Westwood, Michael Wickham, John Wingrove

Introduction

Apart from the heaven-sent provision of food and drink, light was undoubtedly the greatest gift ever bestowed on mankind. A world of twenty-four-hour darkness might have been a marvellous set-up for the Electricity Board, but infinitely wearing on the eyeballs of the rest of us.

Fortunately, we can now have both; natural light and the man-made variety. But people being what they are – inventive, imaginative, ingenious, infuriating – they have to encompass their sources of light with a plethora of decorative devices. A candle on a platter wasn't good enough for our medieval forbears: they had to have cast-iron spikes on stands and the rest. In much the same way in our own time, a simple overhead bulb, or 'naked' bulb, is still not enough for most of us. We have had to invent candle-holders, candelabra, chandeliers, lamp standards as well as all those lights for very particular purposes: desk lamps, dentists' lamps, miners' lamps, stage spotlights, angled lights and so on, ad infinitum.

Most of these decorative devices have not only added to our visual pleasures but also to the quality of light we receive. In much the same way that few people like to read a book in brilliant sunshine without the aid of shaded specs, not many of us like or need unabashed lighting from even a 60-watt bulb. Except for the 3·8 volts, which is about the power of the smallest Christmas tree bulb, most of our lighting needs diffusing or shading. And that's another sphere where the designer comes in. He is not only prepared to design a new-style sconce or standard but also ready and willing to provide just the right shade at just the right angle at just the right height for just the right position.

This book is thus mainly about the work of industrial designers and what has been done to aid our eyes and thus our general well-being in both leisure and working conditions, whether we are orchestra conductors or home-based cooks. You will see here how skilful and ingenious designers have been, whether designing fitments for elegant drawing-rooms or vast drawing-offices. (They are also equally clever at designing lights for underground power plants or overhead gantries, but those matters are outside the province of this essentially domestic primer.)

Here you can look into the variety of lighting available for your living-room, dining-room, bedroom, kitchen and the rest and see the tremendous technical achievements which have been made.

Glowing rectangles of light intimate the pleasure of a well-lit interior

The geometry of lighting

There is no need to live in a Queen Anne mansion or a Brutalist showpiece for lighting to warrant – and reward – considerable time and thought. The interior of almost every house, however unpretentious and run-of-the-mill its exterior, has architectural qualities to be exploited. It has angles, planes and voids in various degrees, shapes and sizes. During the day, these elements form their own patterns, as natural light penetrates from the windows. At night, the pleasant interplay of shadows and pools of brightness is lost. Then it is up to you to make those patterns reappear, in the best possible manner, at the flick of an electric switch.

A room lit by artificial lighting will take on an appearance quite different from its daytime demeanour, so you may need to play around with the geometry of lighting, as well as the geometry of the room, in order to create an interior which provides an individual and agreeable after-dark ambience. Look for the room's good points and make the most of them. If an interior has nothing to distinguish it – which is rare – well-placed lights go a long way towards turning it into something striking.

Natural light

Artists are connoisseurs of daytime lighting, having long since discovered the advantages of northern light in their studios. This may not be the ideal light for the rest of us but, even so, the practical as well as decorative potential of natural light in interior design is often sadly ignored.

But first, attention should be drawn to a few basic points, too often overlooked. A house built with its main rooms to face the sun is lighter (and, incidentally, warmer) than one facing north. Rooms with an open aspect enjoy daylight for longer than rooms facing an enclosed area. Top-floor rooms are brighter than basement ones. Large windows let in more light than small windows. These are some of the ways in which the structure of a house can affect the natural light within it. Some more adventurous modern architects and engineers, unhampered by the old technical limitations on construction and the use of glass, are experimenting in their designs with natural light within a house or flat. Walls are pierced at unexpected angles and heights to bring shafts of decorative sunlight flashing across a room; stairs are lit by low-level panes of glass, and whole walls are glazed so that interiors and exteriors virtually merge into one. But these are rare lighting commodities, although they echo, to some extent, effects produced by that ancient device of the clerestory window.

If you are in the happy position of having a house built to your exact and exacting requirement, you and/or your architect can control

In an open-plan building, the angular lines of the architecture create a multiplicity of light effects. The versatility of natural and artificial light in interiors can be exploited to produce pools of light and shadow, areas of darkness and brightness, dramatic and soft impressions; in fact, they may be channelled to conjure up virtually any mood one wishes to create. Here, the open-planning is accentuated by three round shades suspended at different heights, linking three floors

Rooms unbounded by enclosing walls
enjoy long hours of daylight. Here,
large areas of fixed glazing and glass
doors opening out onto a terrace, break
down the house's limits, affording
increased light and a sense of space.
By night, entertaining out-of-doors
may be illuminated by the lighting
coming from within the house. Design
by Peter Aldington

the architectural elements which, in turn, control the amount of natural
light within the design. But even if you have taken on an existing house,
with every kind of daylight fault, there is a great deal that can be done to
improve its naturally-lit lot.

Providing you have an open mind when it comes to open-plan, some
lighting benefits may be gained by removing all, or part, of an inside
wall, say between a small, dark sitting-room and an unnecessarily bright
dining-room, to make one large, light living area. You could even change
the use of the rooms to get a better disposition of natural light where it is
most needed. There is no reason, for example, why the living-room should
not be moved to the first floor and bedrooms switched to ground level.

A house should have as few areas as possible without a direct source
of daylight, but if there are unavoidably windowless rooms and corridors,
it may be possible to insert an overhead skylight or high-level internal
windows to gain light from one room to another. This is a particularly
useful device to brighten enclosed corridors. The traditional Georgian
fanlight was intended to bring light into the entrance-hall and could well
be copied in more modern designs. Beware, however, of tearing out
small-paned windows from an old house and replacing them with large
sheets of glass. You may improve the light, but you will ruin the façade
in the process.

The interior treatment of a room has considerable effect on its light
values. White and pale colours make a room seem brighter than black
and dark pigments. Shiny surfaces also reflect light. Above all, mirror,
used on a large scale, will apparently and actually increase a room's

natural light. If a window overlooks a confined space, such as a high-walled patio, much can be done to add to the light within the room by painting the garden walls white. Canopies and porches could also be painted white on the underside. Window reveals, too, are perpetrators of gloom unless painted white.

The position of trees and shrubs in the garden can reduce light reaching the interiors of a building to a surprising degree. No one would suggest cutting down a fine old oak, but even quite mature trees can be moved successfully – and not all that expensively – if you follow certain simple but patience-demanding rules. And many an over-profuse ivy or clematis might be trimmed back to advantage.

At the other end of the scale, it has to be acknowledged that there is such a thing as too much light, as anyone living in a west-facing tower block, with vast windows, will confirm. Sun can be a real problem, although here the balance can be redressed more easily than where there is day-long shade. Vertical slatted blinds and Venetian blinds will take the edge off over-bright sunshine and enhance the quality of light by refracting it in different patterns. Sheer curtaining and thin roller blinds diffuse light in a more general way, while exterior awnings, blinds, shutters and *brises soleil* (fixed or free-standing louvred sun-screens) are more major antidotes.

However much you enjoy basking in the sun's rays, never under-estimate their destructive power on furniture. Veneers and antique leather suffer severely under the strain of over-exposure. So, too, do books, records, watercolours, delicate fabrics and some wallcoverings.

Vertical blinds covering the whole window wall can be angled to cut out glare or admit the maximum of light. They give height to this light, airy room, and accentuate its clear-cut lines. Artificial light is concealed in the pelmet above a wall of sliding doors. Two table lamps may be positioned wherever they are needed. The hard-edge painting is lit from below by a spot directed upwards from the floor. Design by Yves Taralon

9

Artificial light

Having satisfied yourself that you have made the best of every available flicker of natural light, you can give full scope to your creative and practical instincts in evolving an artificial lighting scheme which is well up to daytime standards – and possibly better.

There are several types of electric light, each of which has its own distinctive qualities, and these are discussed in the chapter on Technical data, page 76. In addition, there are various possibilities for the positioning of fitments which will also influence the lighting possibilities. Within your master-plan for your lighting set-up, you will need to equate practicality with decorative qualities.

But first things first. Before going all out to obtain interesting lighting

A room on two levels with spotlights set on the edge of the wood ceiling and angled to provide general lighting for both floors. The fireplace in exposed brickwork is sectioned off into storage alcoves lit by spotlights. In the larger, middle recess the various decorative objects are lit up by an angled table lamp. Design by David Thurlow

effects and patterns, you need to be sure that the general level of light in your house or flat is up to a basic minimum. (As a rough guide, the recommended starting-point is 25 watts of lighting for every square metre. Statistics will prove anything, but this is a figure which you ignore at your ocular peril.) In addition, localised areas of light are also needed, either for particular functions or purely for atmosphere.

Experts measure illumination by the concentration of light falling onto a particular surface. Units of light are called lumens (1m) and are calculated per square foot ($1m/ft^2$) or, in metric terms, per square metre (lux). As there are 10·76 square feet to one square metre, one $1m/ft^2$ is equal to 10·76 lux. If you want to be technical about things, here are some recommended figures: bedrooms need the lowest general level of illumination, say 50 lux; stairs, bathrooms and living-rooms need about 100 lux; kitchens and reading areas, 200 lux; workrooms, 400 lux and sewing-rooms, 600 lux.

To calculate these levels of illumination, you multiply the number of lumens per light fitting by the number of fitments. A 100-watt lamp emits 1,260 lumens, a 60-watt lamp 665 lumens. Hence, six bulbs of 100 watts emit 7,560 lumens. This figure, divided by the number of square metres in the room, will give you the lux value.

Overhead lighting

The single, pendant, ceiling light, found in almost all speculatively-built houses, can provide adequate general light in a room, but it rarely comes up to scratch for serious and sustained reading or working, and it leaves a lot to be desired in creating visual interest. If the interiors of your house or flat are lit by this system, and you want to keep to it, then aim for the most splendid and handsome shade you can find. Its shape and material will change the angle, intensity and colour of light emitted, so ask to see a shade when lit before buying. Fortunately, the designs of modern shades are now better and more imaginative than ever before, ranging from colourful Tiffany-style works of art in glass to great spheres of coloured paper, from enamelled metal, plain and patterned, to unashamedly flowery fabrics. There are also some magnificent modern glass chandeliers, ideal for a large, high room. A very low pendant light, provided it is encompassed by a huge shade, can be a startlingly effective focal-point, but it needs to be out of the way of passers-through. A rise-and-fall mechanism, particularly in a dining-room, will add interest, as the level of light can be altered at will, with pleasantly changing shadow effect. Pendant lights, used in groups or in different parts of large rooms, are more decorative than a lone luminary struggling against the odds, but achieving this arrangement may involve rewiring and redecoration.

An excellent alternative to the single pendant light, and one which avoids the agonies of rewiring, is electrified-track lighting, which has a handsome sculptural quality, well suited to modern rooms. It is a highly flexible system in that each track uses a single ceiling point, but allows several spotlights to be fixed along its length and pointed in whichever direction you wish. Usually of aluminium, the track is either recessed into the ceiling, fixed onto the surface or even suspended below it. It is made in several lengths – up to 3·81 metres (12 ft 6 ins) – and can be arranged in any pattern, providing the maximum load for each track

Two small, dark rooms have been converted into a large airy one by removing the wall between them, opening out the staircase and creating a large picture-window at the far end overlooking the garden. Spotlights on a ceiling track are a versatile form of lighting and can be fitted with dimmers to increase the range of effects which can be achieved

A glazed ceiling opens out this hallway and clearly lights up the steps. By night, paintings and sculptures are illuminated by spots set into the wall outside the house. Design by Richard Rogers, N & W Foster

does not exceed 5 amps or 1,200 watts. (If connected to a power point, each track can take up to 16 amps.)

Downlighters are also good overhead lights, but they are at their most effective when seen in groups, and therefore call for more than one ceiling point. This may involve some redecoration if you are thinking of installing them in an existing structure. These spotlights have tall, cylindrical shades, about 230 mm (9 ins) high, with various finishes for particular effect and angles of light. They can be recessed into the ceiling (especially useful if you want to lower a high room by inserting a false ceiling) or project down into the room, partially or wholly.

Wall lighting

Many houses, especially if built between the wars, have points for wall lights, not always in the most predictable and practical places but nevertheless inescapably there. Doing away with them involves a lot of making-good to the decorations, so it may be better economic sense to keep them. In any case, wall lights provide a good general light and can also be made to give some interesting effects.

If you have a traditional interior, there is any number of sconces and wall brackets to choose from. A modern interior, which relies on simple, uncluttered lines for its success, is more difficult to cope with, as wall brackets can prove something of an irritating interruption on a plain white wall, unless perfectly poised, aesthetically and physically, within the general scheme. Here, more than elsewhere, you need to choose fittings carefully to make sure that they add to the room rather than detract from it. The height of the fittings, as well as the type of shade, regulates the angle and look of the light. Again, test the shade when lit up in the shop before parting with any money.

Lighting track is as useful a system for walls as it is for ceilings. If you are up-dating a bedroom, for example, and have inherited wall points on either side of the bed, vertically-fixed lighting track will give a handsome, modern appearance.

Table lamps

Desk lights are needed above all for practicality, as reading and writing both need to be well lit. It is common medical knowledge that bad lighting inhibits concentration and can also lead to eye-strain with consequent headaches. Children doing homework and adults working at home should be provided with lighting at least as good as one would hope to find in an office.

Small, directional spotlights are compact and efficient, but it is important that their light does not appear in too great a contrast with the surroundings, otherwise glare will result. Some people prefer to work by the light of a filament bulb, well shaded, on a hinged or bendable arm. As the light is sited in close proximity to the work, a 40- or 60-watt bulb is probably sufficient. A more highly powered bulb can be dazzling.

Table lamps, which are designed to be decorative rather than a source of light for working by, are excellent for providing a dash of vitality to a lighting scheme. They also supply a reasonable light for occasional reading, and create a pleasant glow beneath pictures. The height of the base alters the type and amount of light, but it is the shades

that are all important as they can make or break the *mise en scène*. Too large and they take over; too small and they look mean; too shapely and they look fussy. Texture, colour and thickness of shades can wreak havoc on light.

Floor lamps
The old-style, large-shaded, standard lamp seems to be going out of favour – and with some reason. Generally speaking, it is no great beauty, is inclined to be in everyone's way and is thus in constant danger of being toppled. The new floor lamps are more practical, having one or more spotlights mounted on a pole of narrow section. The designs are unobtrusive, compact and efficient for working, reading and sewing by.

Some modern floor lamps are more like dramatic pieces of sculpture, in which case all the practical rules are up-ended and their decorative value is obviously more important than their function.

Light sculptures
Light sculptures are not intended to provide an extensive and practical beam, more to show what can be done with light as an art-form. These come in many shapes, from clusters of glistening fronds changing colour and gently swaying in every passing zephyr, to whole coffee-tables which light up with brilliant gashes of fluorescent colour. Special light-units can be bought to project moving colours and shapes onto a screen or wall, like an ever-changing abstract painting.

Glass doors and skylight admit plenty of natural light into this dining-hall. The clean, sculptural lines of the room are complemented by simple lighting fitments – spots set into the ceiling or angled on a track. The turn of the stairs is lit by a separate small spotlight

13

Around the house

The first house to have full electric lighting was *Cragside,* a vast and mysterious pile on an imposing Northumbrian site, designed by that great Victorian architect, R. Norman Shaw for Sir William Armstrong. Lord Armstrong made his fortune in armaments but he was also a compulsive inventor and patron of science, enlisting the aid of his scientist friend, Joseph Swan, to light his newly-built mansion. That was in 1880.

Lighting has come a long way since then and, as every other technological invention, it is improving all the time. Yet it is only comparatively recently that we have seen real flexibility in its application. We can now switch on light which, according to the boffins, is so near real daylight that the very description 'artificial' is almost a misnomer.

So, unless you live in a period house which you intend to furnish and light in true period style (see the chapter on Lighting period houses, page 68), a lighting scheme as modern as the hour is, presumably, your ultimate aim.

The best arrangement is the one which is the most adaptable, allowing for changing mood, function and, to some extent, fashion. It has to take into account, too, the style of the house, shape of the room and depth of your pocket. Each room has its own particular lighting needs; so, too, do its occupants.

Halls, stairs and corridors

The 'traffic' areas of the house – hall, stairs and corridors – are places where many accidents, minor and major, happen. This is due partly to their physical characteristics and partly to the fact that they tend to have poor sources of natural light even at the best of times. Artificial lighting, therefore, should be arranged to minimise the likelihood of any mishaps.

A light near the front door is the first of the hall's requirements. On returning home after dark, you should be able to switch it on even before you have shut the door behind you. Where there is an inner hall, this needs a separate light, possibly operated by a second, two-way switch sited further into the house.

If the hall is very narrow, overhead and wall-mounted lighting are both economical on space. Two or more ceiling or wall points will be needed. A wider hall might include a table for the telephone, in which

The different functions of a living-room need to be considered in its lighting arrangements. Here, the daylight flooding in from the window wall is brought even further into the room by the clerestory windows. Numerous ceiling spots accommodate different lighting needs. Design by Pajamies and Salminen

Above The brightness of this dazzling entrance hall is achieved as much by the lighting employed as by the choice of clear, sharp colours. Glistening reflective finishes are used for the walls, and the ceiling is covered with a sheet of steel. A spotlight set into the ceiling above a nest of tables and a central cylindrical light are fitted with dimmer controls to increase their range of effects. Design by Robin Anderson

Opposite The soft lighting in this living-room is produced by spots mounted in the ceiling and on the beams. The lights can be angled to highlight various features of the room. Concealed lighting makes a feature of the sloping ceiling. By day, the windows set into the ceiling and the glass wall, its panels strongly defined by the L-shaped glazing bars which continue the line of the beams, allow natural light to flood in. Architect Bryan Thomas

case a desk lamp or compact standard lamp is essential to light up dialling and close-printed directories. Be sure that there is a socket to plug this into, plus a second one for connecting up such household appliances as a vacuum cleaner.

Unless some decorative ingenuity is exercised, corridors are usually too long, too high and too narrow to be visually pleasing. This is one area where lighting can do a lot to improve the looks of the interior as well as play its more practical role. A false ceiling with recessed downlighters helps to correct poor proportions and provide excellent light. Different types of cylinders will give various effects. Wall fitments which do not project overmuch, and which are shaded to throw light downwards, also appear to 'lower' the corridor, so long as they are placed at a fairly low level. Spotlights, set at various points and angles, also produce interesting geometric light patterns in a confined space. If you are happy with the proportions of the corridor, then ceiling-mounted, electrified-track lighting is an appropriate choice as it follows the line of this non-room. This type of lighting could also be suspended by several centimetres if the height of the corridor is somewhat awesome and the spots angled to form interesting light patterns.

A change of level along a dark corridor must always be pointed up by the lighting. One good answer is to recess lights into the riser of the step itself. Another is a spotlight specifically directed onto the step. A similar treatment, high up, for changes in ceiling-level might save tall visitors from painful blows.

Most corridor accidents are collisions between one person walking through the area and a second person coming round a corner or out of a room, so make sure that exits and entrances are well lit.

A night-light in a bedroom corridor is advisable if there is a baby in the family who may need attention during the night, or a child who is frightened of the dark but old enough to get out of bed while the rest of the household is asleep. These lamps are of very low wattage – 15w, usually – and are inexpensive and safe to leave on for many hours at a time.

Stairs are the greatest of the traffic-area risks. Serious tumbles can happen here, particularly to older people unsteady on their feet and with less-than-perfect eyesight. Light is needed most near the stair-treads, but it is almost never focused there. Ideally, general lighting should be supplemented by lighting fixed at skirting level, recessed into the risers or concealed under a wall-mounted banister rail. General lighting is best supplied by pendant fittings (at various levels down the whole of the stair-well) or by wall brackets.

At least two two-way switches are needed for the stair-lighting system – one at the bottom and another at the top of the flight. If there is a landing, it may even be worth having a separately switched fitting here which could be left on during the evening if needed. Certainly, a plug socket should be sited on a large landing.

Living-rooms

Nowadays, most living-rooms are just what their name suggests. They are family rooms, coping with every kind of person and activity, from grandparents reading the paper to children playing with their newest

continued on page 33

Rooms built on two levels:
Opposite The short end of an L-shaped room tucked underneath a gallery makes a comfortable enclosed sitting area. The studio sited above takes full advantage of good lighting provided through the skylight. Natural light is amplified on both levels by long rectangular windows. Spotlights are mounted on the beams; cascades of leaves and pot plants combine to bring the garden indoors. Design by Edward Lloyd

Above Cool, sculptural lines of the room are emphasised by four large uncluttered windows, two on each level, sited in the angle of two walls. Neutral colour and large window panes combine to give an appearance of brightness and airy spaciousness. Design by Tullio, Fabio and Alvise Rossi

This page More light has been gained in this restored Tuscan farmhouse by the removal of the roof. Instead of adding conventional windows, a slice of strictly squared glazing was built into the full height of the local stone wall, rising up above the old warmly-coloured roof tiles, into pyramid-like points. Design by Piero Frassinelli, Superstudio

Opposite Sense of space in the living-room has been increased by the addition of a large skylight. Artificial light is provided by spots set into the rim of the skylight and by the sculpture-like curved lamp. Chrome-yellow and white details create a bright, airy feel. Design by Terence and Lynn Trickett

Above Vertical blinds are both
decorative and practical. Easily
rotated or angled in any direction,
they diffuse and control natural
light. Here, they are used to
underline the cool theme of an
uncluttered room. Design by Studio LD

Opposite Graded blue curtains
filter the light and add a softening
touch to the severity of the furniture.
Adjustable spotlights are mounted on
a stand. Design by Bernard Morel

Overleaf Shiny surfaces reflect
light. Here, two highly glossed
ceilings, one white, one pale green,
mirror the bright objects and light
sources in the room below

Left Natural light is admitted through
large, white-shuttered windows;
artificial light is provided by spotlights
set into the ceiling. Design by
Max Clendinning

Right The glossy effect here is
achieved by sanding between layer
after layer of paint. Spots set on an
elaborate track and table lamps
illuminate the interior. Design by
Eric Lieuré

Above Spots set on a track illumine the dining-table, a spiral staircase, and highlight rows of books. The dazzling magenta and black rug is set off by the white walls and pale wood floor. Design by Green, Lloyd and Adams

Opposite Rectangular spots provide the main light sources in a large sitting-room, and are used to create dramatic lighting effects. Perspex light boxes built into the gleaming white shelving give a soft, diffused glow. The inky-black floor finish makes a strong contrast. Design by Robin Anderson

Above Red-lacquer showcases fit neatly into the shape of this octagonal dining-room. Side lighting is used to illumine the seashore treasures. Design by Alberto Pinto

Above right Sitting-room in a converted attic. The storage unit wall houses display alcoves for small items of sculpture, warmly lit from above by strip-lighting. Decorator Isabelle Hebey

Right In a traditional room, a display unit has been created in the recess next to the fireplace. Small spotlights are fitted behind the pelmet which matches the original moulding. Design by Michel Pignères

Opposite The feeling of spaciousness in this living-room is arrived at by linking upper and lower floors by wells of light; there is a void sited over part of the seating area and a grille let into the ceiling above the fireplace. Wall-mounted spots provide additional lighting and may be used for general as well as display purposes. Design by Giulio Savio

Above Medieval flagstoned floor, massive stone fireplace and table form a striking alliance with the delicately sculpted lines of the steel chandelier and curved tulip chairs. Design by Christophe Gevers

Left Spherical pendant light suspended above the dining-table echoes the chrome-yellow theme of the adjoining kitchen. Design by Harry Teggin and David Taylor

Opposite Boldly swirling Art Deco style ceiling constructed in glass, steel and plastic, conceals built-in lighting. Circular skylight is cleverly accommodated in the curves. Design by Diambra Gatti

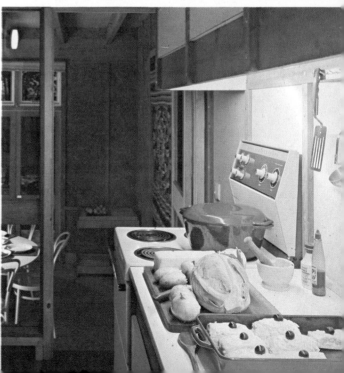

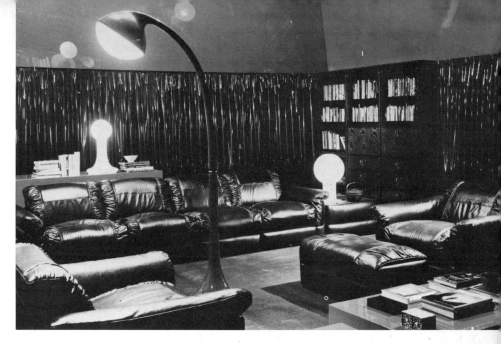

Right The rich, sombre library/
living-room is enlivened by a standard
lamp and sculptural table lamps, all
curves and spheres. Light is reflected
in the shiny vinyl wall hangings.
Design by Olive Sullivan

Several solutions to the problems
posed in kitchens and kitchen/
dining-rooms are shown opposite

Top left Mushroom bulbs fitted into
this curving steel chandelier-like
centre fitment illumine the working
and dining surfaces beneath

Centre A working surface is clearly lit
by strip-lighting fitted beneath a
storage shelf

Bottom left The ideal combination
of tungsten, fluorescent and spotlighting. Three large, non-glare,
bulb-shaped lamps grouped together
form the main light source, while
strip-lighting concealed above the
working surface is both cool and
shadow-free. The storage unit is
highlighted by a flexible system of
spots set on a track suspended from
the ceiling

Top right A tiny one-roomed flat in
Milan is lit by an overhead row of
cylindrical-shaped lights cut off at a
directional angle

Bottom right A concealed fluorescent
strip provides far-reaching lighting
for this small, French kitchen.
Design by Marcial Echenique

continued from page 16

box of poster-paints. Teenagers, young married couples and middle-
aged parents all make demands on this room and therefore want it to be
an agreeable background for their hobbies, friends, television programmes and books.

It stands to reason that with such a diversity of activity, generation
and temperament, all existing within the same four walls, lighting needs
to be, above all, flexible.

A living-room will usually have been built with a single overhead
light which is not ideal, as it can be an irritant if too bright and not
practical if too dim. If you're stuck with such a light, try to back it up
with some more imaginative lighting. Table lamps and standard lamps
will not cause any rewiring and will transform a predictable and pedestrian
lighting scheme into something far more exciting and pleasant to live with.
With this arrangement, you can afford to have a fairly low-wattage bulb,
well-shaded, overhead. This will provide sufficient light on entering the
room, but can be left on or turned off at will when the other forms of
lighting are brought into play.

Another simple improvement is to fix electrified-track lighting, with
spotlights controlled by a dimmer-switch. Straight away, you'll have an
exotic and highly practical lighting scheme. Even this, however, needs
some extras.

To decide what sort of lighting arrangement is needed in your living-
room you have to be fairly objective about yourself and your family.
Most domestic lives fall into a pattern, so it's a matter of trying to detect
it. The sort of questions you need to ask yourself are: Where do we usually
sit? Where do we write letters? Pay bills? Do homework? And what about
reading the paper and looking up radio and television programmes?
Which pictures are special favourites? Are there any pieces of china and
glass that would look particularly well if lit up at night? What sort of
atmosphere do we want to create? These are all questions that a lighting
designer would ask you, so if you're doing the scheme yourself, you
might as well be as professional about it as possible.

The size and character of your family will determine, to some extent,
the type and quantity of light. If you have very young children who have

nowhere else to play on rainy days than in the living-room, give china table lamps a miss. If there are much older people in the house, remember that extra light will be needed for reading and so on. The eyes of a sixty-year-old man or woman may need up to twice as much light to function at the same efficiency level as those of a ten-year-old.

As a guide, an average-sized living-room needs two ceiling points (this will allow for a far more pleasant general light than a single point) and one or two points on two of the walls. In addition, double sockets are needed, preferably on all four walls, for table lamps and floor lamps. These do not have to be sited near the corners. In fact, if you are quite sure where furniture and desk lights are to be placed, it may be more convenient to have sockets positioned nearer these in order to avoid long lengths of flex.

Large living-rooms, for instance over 5·49 metres (18 ft) square, will need more lighting. Anything up to four ceiling points will not be too much. Table lamps or wall lighting will be needed, especially if the room's length is much greater than its width, so make allowance for two points on two walls. Very long walls will probably benefit from more than one set of double sockets. After all, it's far better to find there are too many than too few sockets. Generally, these should be placed 150–200 mm (6–8 ins) above floor level.

Above The ceiling in this airy living area has been lowered to contain concealed downward lighting at its edges. Above the windows light is thrown upward from behind the pelmet. Design by Stout and Litchfield

Opposite Glass doors linking a hallway and living-room are a simple device for increasing the spaciousness and lightness of both. Inverted, torch-shaped lamps suspended from the ceiling can provide dramatic lighting of plant forms. A mushroom table lamp and curving standard lamp are adaptable, multi-purpose lighting appliances. Design by Yves Ruhlmann

Workrooms necessitate careful lighting if eye-strain is to be avoided. Over-bright natural light can be controlled and diffused through translucent blinds. For close work, a caterpillar-like bending lamp is fitted to the edge of the desk

Workrooms

Even if you don't do much desk-work at home, you still have bills to settle and letters to write. A good general light is necessary, just as it is in any room, but a desk light or table light is essential. It should throw a good, direct light onto the surface of the table, book or paper without creating glare. The light should be well shaded so that none shines in your eyes and for this reason, pale coloured, thin shades are not suitable, nor are open-top designs. Directional desk spotlights are efficient, although some people find the contrast they create between the area they illuminate and the rest of the room is uncomfortable. Good general lighting will lessen this. Some of the decorative, modern table lamps, which have a gentle light permeating from the whole form, look attractive but can be tiring to read by, unless the top half of the shade is darker and virtually opaque.

A balanced, hinged-arm design takes a lot of beating at a desk, but remember that the main source of light should come from the left-hand side as you write (or from the right if you are left-handed); otherwise, your arm will cast a shadow on your work.

One of the better designs of modern desk lighting has a long, low, horizontal shade, like a trough, which directs light downwards over a

Daylight filters through vertical blinds
set against exposed stone walls.
Overhead, light boxes are recessed
into the ceiling. Desk surface is clearly
lit by a movable spherical bulb on a
stand. Design by Guy Chansioux

wide area of the table-top. Spurn any design with holes in the shade,
however diminutive, through which light can escape, as these specks of
brilliance can become irritating spots before the eyes.

Some people find that low standard lamps, particularly the modern
spotlit versions, are excellent to read or knit by. These can be positioned
with the light coming from over your left shoulder, so that the work in
hand is perfectly illuminated. Some of the designs have a single spot on
a thin pole, well weighted for stability. Others have two or more spots,
all of which can be raised or lowered on the pole, as well as swivelled in
different directions. These lamps do, however, generate a certain amount
of heat, and are dazzling unless placed well behind you.

Schoolchildren do an enormous amount of reading and writing,
which can be a strain even on the most youthful of eyes if not provided
with adequate lighting. Many hours of winter homework are done after
dark, so good general lighting and a desk light are extremely important.

Do-it-yourself work needs a good general light, which is best provided
by a fluorescent tube, with the addition of a sturdy directional lamp for
detailing, such as the traditional angled lamp, possibly clamped to the
edge of the toolbench. If you choose some form of wall-mounted spotlight,
make sure it is one that remains 'cool'. So long as the handywork is being
carried out away from the living-rooms, fluorescent lighting is ideal.

Dining-rooms

Anyone who has eaten in a badly-lit restaurant – and, alas, there are too many of them – will know just how much lighting affects one's enjoyment of food, whether it is a hamburger and chips or *filet de boeuf en croûte*. If hunger has dimmed all visual senses, no one is going to bother about his surroundings, but thanks to the affluent, well-fed society, most diners-out need more than just a plateful of whatever is going. Appetites and taste-buds respond to a certain amount of visual cosseting.

The same principles apply at home, whether you are eating *en famille* or have invited a dozen people to a dinner-party. The lighting should be sufficiently flexible to suit both situations equally well.

In a dining-room, or dining area, lighting is, in the main, seen from a seated position, so the scheme should be worked out with this in mind. A light hung very low over the table looks attractive but its height, bulb and shade must be selected with care to ensure that glare does not become uncomfortable. Choose a pearlised bulb which softens the

Right A recessed light above the entrance to the dining-room prevents the risk of collisions. Within the room, a horizontal ceiling track with spots set above the dining-table can provide varied lighting effects. Design by Robin Anderson

Opposite above Circle upon circle is the theme of this dining area, from the round, glass table to the relief map feel of the ceiling, with its built-in 360° of light

Below This dining corner is cheerfully lit by a single pendant lamp

quality of the light, for if it is too bright, there will be some unpleasant shadows and some harsh outlines. A high-level, ceiling-hung light, undimmed and glaring everyone in the face, is not a good arrangement. A rise-and-fall fitting gives some flexibility in solving this problem, as you can find out for yourself what level is best for light and atmosphere. This is a simple means of changing an interior from a day-to-day family room into a dramatic setting for a party. Dimmer-switches are also useful for this purpose.

Getting light away from the table altogether can prove successful. Low-level table lamps and fittings placed against the walls of the room throw a flattering light from behind the diners. They also have the effect of enlarging the room by 'painting' its perimeters lighter than the centre, as well as showing up pictures and other peripheral points of interest.

If you opt for table lamps (and these are particularly appropriate in a traditionally-furnished room), the choice of shade is as important as the decorative value of the base and the suitability of the light-bulb. Dead-white shades give a harsher light than duller and darker colours.

A glittering chandelier can look pretty in a traditional dining-room, but care must be taken that it doesn't overburden diners with light and too formal an atmosphere. Spotlights, well dimmed and well directed, are, as always, a flexible means of lighting.

Right Storage cabinet lighted from within is both decorative and practical. A steel hood above the hob built into the island unit houses several downlighters

Below Shadow-free strip-lighting fitted beneath a storage cabinet clearly illuminates the working surface. Translucent panels covering the ceiling conceal tubes of diffused fluorescent light, providing good general lighting

Kitchens

Artificial lighting in the kitchen needs more imagination and skill than in any other room in the house. It is usually 'fixed' – no standard and table lamps here – and therefore comparatively inflexible. Yet it has to be truly effective in every corner, both for working by and for safety, as well as create a pleasant interior in which to spend many wintry hours preparing the meals for family and friends.

The usual work pattern in a kitchen is: store, prepare, cook, wash, store. Each process needs adequate lighting, natural or artificial. Make sure that one stage is not lit up to the disadvantage of another. It is dangerous to find you are standing in your own light in front of a stove, and you are likely to double the number of breakages at the sink if everything is dimmed by your own shadow.

A sound arrangement is a combination of tungsten, fluorescent and spotlighting. The first provides a pleasant general light, especially if the kitchen is also used for eating. The second, if it is well integrated into the design of the room, is excellent for lighting up work surfaces and, so long as the area is limited, the rather stark quality of the light will not spoil the ambience. The third can be directed into awkward corners.

An all-spotlight scheme may look and work well in a large kitchen but, in a confined space, ordinary spots can generate too much heat for the chef's comfort. These 'warm' light-sources can make life difficult for any would-be cool-and-collected hostess who may find herself working at a hot stove while being subjected to a battery of arc lights. There are special dichroic 'cool' spots available which are preferable.

Most modern kitchens have two banks of storage units, one set on the floor and the other wall-hung. This is an ideal arrangement for lighting, as small fluorescent strips can be concealed on the underside of the wall units, thus lighting up the work surface below. As the lights are close to the worktop, they can be so low-powered that even people who are anti-fluorescent should not find them unpleasant. Tungsten filament strip-lights could be substituted, however, and both varieties are usually operated by cord pull-switches, making them independent of the switch for the main light.

Fluorescent lighting enjoyed a great kitchen boom when it first appeared on the domestic market, as it provides a cool shadow-free, far-ranging light. Alas, though, it also tended to destroy the character of the room and either looked depressingly cold or unnaturally rosy, depending on the colour of the tube. Bafflers undoubtedly improve the quality of light, and many people find this a good system to work by, so if the kitchen is used only for cooking, there is something to be said for it. If the kitchen doubles as a family dining area, some sort of lighting compromise is called for, using spots or tungsten lighting at least near the table.

A complete ceiling of diffused fluorescent light undoubtedly provides a good general light, technically speaking. The tubes are hidden behind translucent panels which are supported by a criss-cross framework. If you like fluorescent light to cook by, this is not unpleasant and the squared-up effect of the structure can look quite handsome.

Deep cupboards and larders need to be lit from within. A time-switch or door-operated switch guarantees that there is no waste of electricity if the door is shut and the light left on.

This long, narrow kitchen has lighting concealed above the work surfaces. Strip-lighting is far-reaching and cool, essential in a room which can quickly become intolerably hot. Overhead lighting is kept to a minimum, a single circular light being fitted over the door. Note the glazed panel at the side of the door. Design by Westwood, Piet and Partners

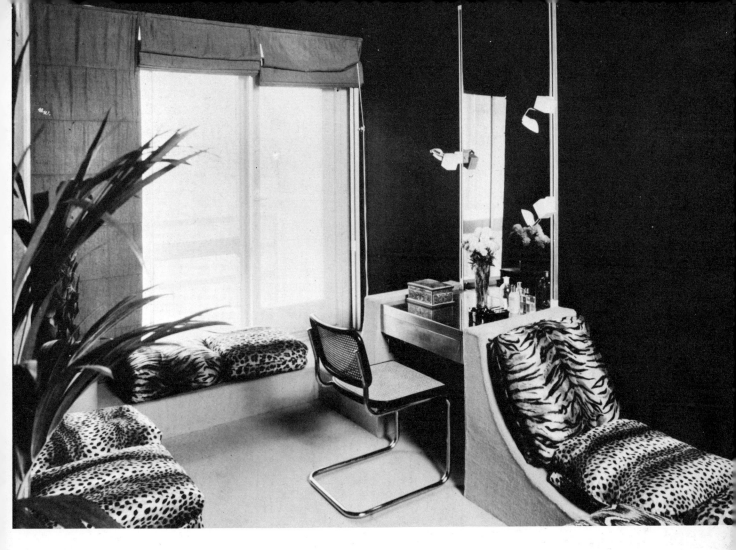

Bedrooms

The quality of light in a bedroom is of paramount importance, not just to coerce insomniacs into the right frame of mind for a good night's sleep, but to create a restful retreat from the humdrum hustle of the day. Any jarringly-bright lights are out – or should be.

The single ceiling pendant is at its least successful here, unless warm-toned and well shaded. A more scattered arrangement is far more suitable for these rooms. General lighting is only the start, however, as other forms of light are needed in specific areas. The bed and dressing-table, for example, should have their own luminary sources.

A single bed requires a single bedside light. A double bed or twin beds means doubling up on the lighting. If two people share a bedroom, but only one likes to read in bed, this requires some harmonious planning. Obviously, he or she wants enough light to be able to follow the plot of the latest Simenon thriller, but this can be enfuriating to any would-be sleeper alongside. Small, movable-arm spotlights are practical compromises, although they can be tiring on the eyes as they produce a small vivid area of light which throws the white paper of the book into unpleasant contrast with the darkness of the room.

If neither party reads in bed, then low-wattage bedside lighting gives a more restful feeling. This could be in the shape of pendant lights, hung low and near to the wall on either side of the bed, or wall brackets.

Above A full-length mirror visually enlarges this exotic bedroom. Vertical tracks on either side carry directional spots. Natural light is filtered through translucent curtains, or can be virtually blocked out by heavy blinds. Design by David Resnick Associates

Opposite This up-dated four-poster bed has spots angled from either side on adjustable vertical tracks. The curtained window wall has concealed lighting built into the pelmet. Design by Robin Anderson

Above Large, egg-shaped table lamps on either side of a double bed are reflected in the richly lacquered walls

Opposite Bedroom with built-in bathroom has curves and circles as its dominant theme. It cleverly incorporates a lighting recess into the curve of the wall. Spots recessed into the ceiling can be controlled to produce varied lighting effects

Table lamps look decorative but have disadvantages in that they can be knocked over, a problem which can be solved if lighting is fixed onto the headboard. Spots on vertical electrified track are versatile modern equivalents of traditional brackets but, as with all wall-mounted lighting, they make for difficulties if you have a sudden whim to move the furniture around.

Lighting for a dressing-table needs to be as efficient as you dare make it. If you can face up to the face before you, then take a few tips from theatrical people and light it up to the maximum. Light should come from in front of your face, not from behind your head. If it is concentrated in one area, there will be an impossible amount of glare to cope with. Lighting placed on either side of a large mirror, in the best backstage manner, is undoubtedly the most successful arrangement. Two ceiling pendants, hung on either side of the person seated at the dressing-table is a good second-best. These should be slightly higher than, and in front of, the face.

Walk-in clothes cupboards are a rare luxury, but deep, non-walk-in cupboards are more common, especially in older houses. Both these storage units are far more practical if well lit. This is the one and only area of the bedroom complex which could take a fluorescent light. Its value here is that it is a 'cool' light, thus reducing the risk of scorching, or worse, any fabric that may accidentally come into contact with it and, provided that you choose the right tube, you will have near-perfect light for colour matching. To ensure that the light is not left on accidentally when the cupboard is shut, it should be operated by the door mechanism.

Bathrooms

It has taken a long time for many people to tear themselves away from their traditionally austere approach to the bathroom. Even those who flaunted their comforts elsewhere in the house seemed to think that any hint of bathroom luxury was a sure sign of moral and physical decadence. Now, fortunately, all that is changing. We can buy baths in every colour of the rainbow, as well as in some decidedly self-indulgent shapes; tiles and water-resistant wallcoverings have never before been patterned in so many different and coloured ways; we can even buy deepest-pile carpet to cushion the wettest of feet.

Lighting, however, is one area of bathroom design which has not kept pace with the rest. Its progress may have been hampered by all the safety regulations which, quite rightly, limit the use of electricity in this room. It may have been slowed down too, by the fact that many people think the large cost of redecorating and rewiring an existing bathroom, particularly if it is tiled from floor to ceiling, is disproportionate to the resulting luminous benefits.

You're lucky if you have a bathroom still at the planning stage, whether you're having a house built or doing a transformation job to an old one. There are several ways of lighting a bathroom so that it is safe but is something more than a squared-up box of purely functional activity. Long flexes, exposed wiring, standard lamps, flimsy fittings, internal switches and materials that easily rust are all unsuitable for the bathroom, but that doesn't mean that the scheme has to be dull. Downlighters, recessed in the ceiling, for example, give an attractive atmosphere to the room at night and are practical for angling over particular areas for shaving and reading. Lighting concealed behind false cornices or panels in the walls are other interest-giving devices.

But what can be done to improve the lighting in an existing bathroom without going to vast expense? First of all, if there is a single ceiling point (which, once again, is the standard arrangement), make sure that the bulb, or bulbs, you use are bright enough. That's not to say, of course, that it should be a harsh light, but a filament bulb of 40 or 60 watts cannot provide an adequate light either for safety or for making-up. Use a 100-watt bulb, with a 'pearl' finish, for the best effect.

A pendant fitting is far from ideal for the bathroom. It is better to choose a ceiling-mounted one with a glass or plastic shade which does not cut out too much light. It should also have rust-proof fittings and be easily demounted for cleaning.

If you choose a fluorescent light for the bathroom, again be sure the fittings are rust-proof, as steam can be very corrosive to the contacts and even diminish the life of the tube. The colour of the tube depends on the colour of the bathroom. Generally speaking, 'natural' is a good choice as it comes nearest to daylight on a fine day, but 'de luxe warm-white' may be more flattering in an all-white interior. In any case, don't leave the tube exposed to view. It needs to be well baffled, as fluorescent light does not have the soft quality of tungsten.

If the bathroom is to be used for making up, really good lighting is needed by the mirror. As for the dressing-table lighting in the bedroom,

Above Large-scale lighting in a narrow, tiled bathroom. Panels containing tubes of fluorescent light run the length of the wash basin unit, while light boxes recessed into the wood-panelled ceiling give a good general light. Design by Clyde Rich

Opposite The circular sweep of the bath is echoed in the two mirrors with cylindrical lights above. Similar lamps are suspended from the ceiling for overall lighting. White carpeted flooring, in contrast to the dark walls, increases the brightness of the room

a fitting on either side of the mirror is better than one overhead. These mirror lights can be operated by the main switch as well as by an independent cord switch. Strip-lights, specially designed for shaving by, are available with a socket incorporated for an electric razor.

A useful source of additional heat for a bathroom is found in the combined heater/lighting fitting. This is ceiling-mounted, as a pendant fitting, and can be used either as a light by itself in summer or in winter as a heater – or both if it's dark as well as cold. It must be connected to the ring circuit as the loading is too great for the lighting circuit. This form of lighting, available with fluorescent or tungsten lamps, is practical but the fittings themselves are rarely handsome to look at.

A complete ceiling panel of fluorescent light is another possibility, as it is in the kitchen, but on its own it does not provide much visual interest from the point of view of light patterns.

Children's rooms

Teenagers' rooms are lit along much the same lines as their adult counterparts. Small rooms need good general lighting provided by one ceiling point or two wall points; larger rooms will need more. In addition, a light next to the bed is an obvious requirement, whether wall-fixed or free-standing on a table; so, too, is a desk lamp if the room is used for studying. Games rooms are like lions' dens as far as lighting is concerned. Make sure that all bulbs are well protected from table-tennis bats being flailed over-enthusiastically.

Younger children can't be trusted with electricity, so lighting needs to be as straightforward as possible and well out of reach. Yards of snaking flex and flimsy table lamps are dangerous. Even a bedside light is safer if set on the wall.

Many infants like the reassurance of a night-light. This uses a 15-watt bulb and is inexpensive to run. It also has the advantage of providing sufficient light for a parent to check that all is well in the nursery without having to turn on the main beam.

A new form of low-intensity nursery lighting is the electro-luminescent night-light. In the form of a 'glowing' picture, its running costs are minimal.

Above The bedroom is lit by adjustable spots on vertical tracks. Directional lights are set at the side of the mirror and in the dressing alcove

Above left and opposite Two opulent bedrooms designed by Max Clendinning. The smaller, with its striking red mock-canopied bed, is illuminated by a ring of light set into the ceiling, and by two round bedside lamps. The larger room continues the theme of circles and employs concealed lighting set into an orangey-red circular recess in the ceiling, controlled by dimmers. Two directional spotlights with dimmers and a bedside lamp provide light for reading

Left This brilliantly glowing interior is achieved by reflective, lacquered walls and a scatter of neon-coloured cushions. Spots on a horizontal track afford flexible lighting effects. The table lamp provides a sculptural corner-piece. Design by Eric Lieuré

Opposite below left Individually controlled lamps are positioned above the bed for reading. Metal table lamps, their shades like upturned pots, may be used to read or work by. Design by Lars and Maria Knutsson

Below right Bathroom lighted Hollywood-style by a row of bulbs set above a long rectangular mirror

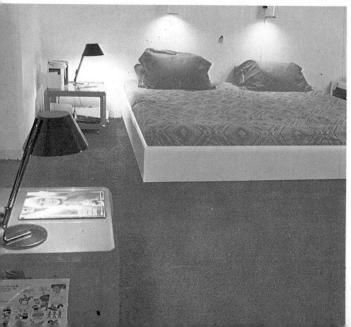

Glazed bays and sliding partitions
make this apartment highly flexible
in its layout. An open, versatile space
such as this necessitates a lighting
system equal to its flexibility

Above The bedroom area has spotlights
angled on a vertical track beside the

bed, and concealed lighting between
full-length cupboards

Opposite The main living space
continues the cool, light theme of
neutral tones; beige and creamy-white.
A staggered system of shelving is
built on the movable living-room wall,

and houses strips of lighting to illuminate various *objets d'art*. The edges of the room are painted by light concealed in the pelmets, while a picture recess is lighted from above by a single spot. A fine-stemmed standard lamp lights up the terrace. Design by Maurice Bentz

Left Ill-lit staircases are hazardous. Here, spotlights set into the risers light up the darkly carpeted steps in a colourful Italian flat

Top An open staircase is richly lit by a cascade of glittering, golden bulbs. Design by François Catroux

Above Strip-lighting along the staircase wall is neat and efficient

Opposite above left The stairway is clearly lit by a row of spherical spots fitted to a track on the ceiling and reflected in the glossy walls

Above right A new slant on strip-lighting. A band of light is sandwiched between the shiny plastic and chrome of the banister rail. The clear-cut simplicity complements the clean, elegant lines of the room below. Additional light is provided by a curvaceous light sculpture and overhead spots. Design by John Michael

Right Two views of a staircase lighted by a direct overhead fitment. Note the illuminated display niches in the curve of the stairwall and the spot directed towards the telephone table

These three photographs show
several new designs, some French,
some Italian, which fulfil a
multitude of lighting needs

Opposite The centre light fitment of
three glass spheres containing silvered
bulbs is in a living-room designed by
Giuliana Corsini

Above A table lamp, reading light and
standard lamp are in a bedroom by
François Catroux

Right A curved table lamp is in a
hallway designed by Karl Lagerfeld

Above Natural light in this simple
black and white interior is filtered
through full-length curtains. Old and
new elements in the room provide
additional light sources. The large
seventeenth-century Venetian mirror
increases the room's natural light,
while artificial light is provided by
a ribbon-like length of tubing which
may be casually piled up or draped
wherever it is needed. Design by
Piero Sadun

Right Ivory-coloured sitting-room
has highly glossed ceiling and walls
reflecting the decorative light sources.
A mushroom-shaped lamp, a coil
of tubing and a hooded steel light
sculpture underline the cool mood of
the room. Additional light is provided
by small table lamps. Design by
Cini Boeri

Left Concealed lighting is built
into the pelmet above gauze-covered
windows. The sculptural table lamp
with its glass, wing-like shade is a
strong focal point at the end of a
long table

The Arco lamp introduced as a
new interpretation of the
traditional standard lamp has been
taken up and developed by many
designers in recent years

Above A spherical bulb forms the
light head of this pendulous lamp
overhanging the dining-table. An
identical head set on a metal stand
comprises the table version. Decorative
glass objects are ideally lit by being
arranged on a free-standing shelving
system placed in front of the window.
Daylight may be controlled and
diffused through translucent blinds

Left Another curving standard
lamp, its perforated shade echoed
in the lattice-backed chairs. The
curvaceous theme is underlined by a
table lamp with a semi-circular
luminous head. Design by
Piero Sadun

Opposite Here, the metal shaded
light depending from a long stem
illuminates the coffee-table area.
A decorative and firm base is provided
by a marble stand. Additional light
in the form of a table lamp set in the
corner and a globe of light above the
fireplace intensifies the warm glow of
the salmon-pink walls and highly
polished floor. Design by Jack and
Barbro Wahl

Three settings where the mood has been altered dramatically by the lighting employed

Left A clinically crisp black and white daylit room is transformed and softened by the use of artificial light. Concealed lighting is built into brown-painted platforms situated behind the sofa unit and banked up against the wall. The light sculpture-cum-coffee-table radiates a blue metallic glow and a tube of light shines from within a spiralling steel sculpture. A warmly lit dining-room opens off the sitting-room. Design by Alberto Pinto

Below left Shadowy foliage pattern projected onto the dining-room wall complements the exotic triptych in silk on the adjacent wall. The two side-pieces fold inwards to form a large circular mirror which visually enlarges the room. The party atmosphere is underlined by lighted candles. Design by Warren Platner

Below and opposite The mood, colour and patterning of two white rooms joined by a framed opening can be changed at will by a battery of coloured lights

Display

Most of us like to live in a house or flat which is something more than a simple shelter from wind and rain. We are naturally acquisitive and enjoy seeing our more decorative belongings about us.

Placing and lighting these objects to advantage doubles our enjoyment of them and enhances the room in general. This is true both during the day, when natural light has to be taken into account, and at night, when artificial light should be made to work for its keep.

However great a work of art may be, it will be lost if not hung in the right place. It needs to have light falling onto its surface without any of that dreaded glare which can obliterate not just small details but whole canvases. (Non-reflective picture glass is available but it tends to soften outlines when seen from certain angles.) A degree of experimenting will be needed to discover exactly where you should hang your pictures. Even the height of a painting can affect its daytime visibility, depending on the position and size of windows.

Many lessons can be learnt from art galleries and museums. (A gallery renowned for the excellence of its natural lighting is the small, unassuming-looking Marianne North building in London's Kew Gardens, designed by James Fergusson in 1882 to house a collection of delightful plant drawings.) Overhead windows or those placed high up provide the best natural light for pictures but curtains, blinds and artificial lighting are all valuable in devising the perfect domestic gallery. If windows are all sited on one wall, that will be the darkest and most lifeless place of all for your lithographs, collotypes or whatever.

Artificial lighting for paintings is far less limiting than natural light, as the whole thing can be under your control. In spite of the plethora of picture-lighting devices, the best system is usually the one that appears to be the most casual and matter-of-fact. Picture lights, fixed to the top of frames, provide effective illumination but they should be used sparingly. These employ tungsten filament bulbs, shaded from above, but unless plugged into a socket immediately behind the picture, they entail a lot of unsightly flex. A flexible system of directional spotlights will achieve much the same results without looking so studied. Light can be thrown onto a picture from quite a distance and, best of all, can be fitted with a special shielding device so that the pool of light is exactly the same area and shape as the picture for which it is designed.

A table lamp placed on a piece of furniture below a painting will bring the latter out of nightly obscurity but it will produce an uneven effect. This may be of little importance if you prefer picture-lighting to look almost accidental within the interior.

To see china at its best during the day, the return wall – that is the one

Above A spotlight recessed into an alcove illuminates life in the fish tank below. Spotlights on a track light the dining area, and can be angled to produce interesting effects on the tree fronds

Opposite In the foreground of this brilliantly colourful living-room on New York's Central Park, large cubes containing giant orange neon coils and white scaffold-like tubes comprise two of Rudi Stern's light sculptures. Others in neon and Plexiglass may be seen around the room. Greens predominate throughout; paintwork, flooring, furniture and foliage. A bright painting and a table, its base a column of light, combine with the other features to generate an atmosphere of exotic exuberance

opposite the window wall – is the best place for its display. Here, shelving, table-tops and mantelpieces will all provide good bases. Walls at right-angles to windows might cause a certain amount of shadowing if the window is directly in line with the display shelves. Recessed shelving along this wall will have increased problems of shade.

Glass is the most difficult of all collections to display during the day. Unless it has good light from behind, much of its beauty is lost. Light from the side will help to some extent, but the solidity of a backing wall will have a somewhat deadening effect. Natural light can be turned to advantage if your glass collection is placed either on glass shelves in front of a window (so long as you don't need to open it), or on a free-standing shelving system placed near a good source of natural light. The window-sill itself is the simplest setting of all, but it may be too low for your collection to be fully appreciated.

Both china and glass benefit enormously from some form of artificial lighting in the evening. Again, a great deal can be discovered by visiting some of the special exhibitions arranged by the museums. The Tutan-khamun exhibition staged at the British Museum, for example, was a masterpiece of display lighting. Though that sort of dramatised arrange-ment is taking things too far at home, there are useful hints to be gleaned.

The colours of patterned porcelain are well able to stand up to this sort of specialised lighting treatment and, indeed, are sadly dimmed if not given it. Glass often comes to life under the penetrating gaze of an electric light in a way that it never does during the day.

If china and porcelain are set on a table-top or commode in a traditional room, a largish table lamp will light the collection from above. Unless you are determined to single out a particular object, then this relaxed approach is effective for a closely-arranged group. Some china cupboards and corner cupboards can take a concealed light. The best place for this is usually just above the door, inside, where it will not be seen and will throw light on the china from the front. Spotlights can also be directed so that collections are bathed in a pool of flattering light.

A recessed shelving alcove, a niche in a fine Georgian mansion, or something simpler and more modern, might also be improved at night if well lit. If the alcove is modern, you could build a piece of false wall or pelmet extending down a few centimetres from the real wall. It is then a simple matter to conceal behind this a narrow strip of light, either tungsten filament or extremely carefully controlled fluorescent.

Ideally, glass should be lit artificially from behind. This makes for problems if the fitting is to be hidden from view which, of course, it should be. However, one solution is to mount the smallest possible spots near the top corners of a rectangular recess.

Statues, large or small, bronze or marble, look dramatic if skilfully lit. Even a luxuriant palm will produce some interesting shadows if a small lamp is placed beneath its leaves.

Sculptures and paintings require carefully planned display lighting. Here, natural light floods in from a window at right angles to the display wall. Excessive shadowing can be compensated by a flexible system of directional spotlights set into the ceiling. This system also provides efficient, unstudied lighting for the paintings. The lower display shelves are brightly illuminated by round, metal table lamps. Design by Pinto

Lighting period houses

A modern house or flat is almost always better lit by and better suited to modern lighting. A period house can be a problem, however, particularly if it is furnished consistently with its style and age. Here, the golden rule – or, at least, silver-gilt rule – is not to be too set on period lighting for these period rooms.

By 'period' in relation to houses and rooms, most people are apt to think of the span between, say, 1500 and 1830. But nowadays, Victorian and turn-of-the-century houses are every bit as period.

It could be argued that the older the house, the more up-to-date the lighting should be. Fifteenth-century candlestands rarely convert well to electricity, and many of the reproduction electric candle-type fitments are too flimsy-looking to be visually pleasing or, indeed, truly appropriate in the rugged settings for which they are made. By all means use original candlesticks and candelabras, complete with real candles, for their decorative value (maybe even for occasional use), but get your evening lighting from more modern fittings, preferably concealed.

The earlier and more beamed a house is, the more 'character' the estate agents will say it has. In one sense they are right, as inglenook fire-places, exposed stone walls and deep window reveals are ready-made adventure-playgrounds for the lighting designer, amateur and professional alike. Well-placed spotlights will create a diversity of interesting effects, as well as provide good, practical light.

But if you insist on having reproduction light fittings wired for electricity, be sure to go to one of the specialist firms which produce these fittings based on original designs. (Clough Williams-Ellis, who has always shown such flair in his work on old houses, used these in the form of huge torchères at Ashridge House in Hertfordshire.) Bulbs for these fittings are usually 'pearlised' and fluted to look like a candle flame. The most splendid of these reproduction torchères measures up to 1 metre (3 ft) high, with bulbs of about 200 mm (8 ins) high. For a gothic castle or medieval manor-house, these are about the best of the reproductions you can get.

In large, eighteenth-century houses, rooms tend to be more straightforward, the proportions pleasant and there may even be some agreeable plasterwork centred on a rose for a chandelier. Unless you live in a *cottage orné* in rustic style, you won't be able to fall back on picture-postcard beams to help you with your lighting effects. Concealed spots on their own are probably not the answer, as period rooms call for appropriate fittings which are not only there but seen to be there. Handsome chandeliers and wall sconces are hard to beat in this type of setting. Again, original fittings are best left as they are, as light-bulbs and shades usually fail to look right on these. Some devious electric lighting is needed in the form of hidden spots. One or more of these can be fixed strategically to a floor or wall position, so that light will play upon the facets of the cut glass or the gleaming brass in a more spectacular way than authentic candles. For your reading, tatting, chess, Scrabble, crosswords and conversation, you can use table lamps which will give your period rooms the pools of light they so emphatically need.

The fact is that there is such infinite scope in the table lamp that it will suit almost all period requirements. After all, the most cherished possession of your eighteenth-century living-room is likely to be an inlaid

Vertical slatted blinds are visually at ease in a period room accommodating modern elements. Natural light is also admitted through tall french windows. Plain-shaded table lamps, small spots angled from the ceiling and ornate candelabra provide general and party lighting

Spotlighting in this living-room throws the beamed ceiling into high relief, and can be used to create a variety of effects. A single, spherical pendant light links the dining- and living-room areas

rosewood sofa table or a beautifully-banded or gadrooned side-table, both of which would make perfect supports for a table lamp with a well-designed shade.

Shades are, of course, a controversial matter. Too many period rooms have been ruined by lush, over-blown, silky, chintzy shades of complex curves and tasselling. Far better to keep to simple shapes of drum section or gently sloping straight sides, and to have a plain linen or lacquered card shade, lined with parchment or similar material.

A large number of Victorian houses still have plasterwork ceiling roses from which was suspended a gas or oil pendant fitting. If you live in such a period piece, then think twice before tearing down these ceiling features. Very often the rooms are high and, like their eighteenth-century predecessors, cry out for a pendant light of some importance. Nineteenth-century lighting was often shaded with opalescent glass and therefore can be converted to electricity without spoiling its appearance. After all, the intrusive light-bulbs will be hidden from view. Old gaseliers convert particularly successfully to electricity, as their hollow branches can incorporate wiring with the greatest of ease, but there are so many good reproduction fittings of the period – wall brackets, reading lamps and ceiling units – that it may not be worth the effort. But choose these copies carefully; avoid anything fussy and lacking in substance.

Even early twentieth-century interiors are now something of a period cult, and there is certainly no shortage of Art Nouveau and Art Deco fittings, original and reproduction. The multi-coloured Tiffany lamps of the twenties and thirties are beautifully attuned to the decorative themes and lighting needs of our own time.

A small but important point in lighting a traditional house is the choice of light switches. In a period room, with brass door furniture, brass chandeliers and brass-framed mirrors, it is a pity not to follow this theme through, as a small square of plastic can become an outsize irritant to a sensitive eye. Black-painted iron switches are best in centuries-old castles, manors and cottages with black-iron light fittings.

Exterior lighting

Outdoor lighting is more than a pretty effect. It is an excellent anti-burglar device and a decorative means of ensuring that you avoid stumbling over stones and other hazards.

A little light goes a long way outside, so there is no need to invest in the sort of arc-lamp set-up used for after-dark football matches. A few, low-level lights, comparatively small but strategically placed, are sufficient to light up most paths, drives and steps. There are several weatherproof designs available, most of which are of the tungsten halogen variety. Steps with lighting recessed in the risers, or in the walls on either side of the flight, are safe and look attractive. Not to be forgotten, however, is a light fitting near the front door, both to light up callers and to help you find the right key and keyhole.

After dark, we lose our sense of colour and we see objects in black and grey only. Pools of artificial outdoor light will bring back colour to the area illuminated, but the further an object is placed from the source of light, the less its colour can be appreciated. Hence, lighting should be concentrated on bold shapes and contours rather than on colours. A flowerbed of low-growing plants, however brilliant an array they present in the midday sun, is disappointing when seen by artificial light. Statues, trees with spreading boughs, stately hollyhocks, cascades and even still ponds of light-reflecting water, all look well when lit up.

Coloured lights are only suitable for flowerless patios with high walls and paving, or for swimming-pools and ponds. In a foliated and floriated setting, lamps of different hues detract from the plants and turn the garden into a fairground of unnatural and garish growth.

Lighting placed underwater, in a swimming pool or small pond, looks delightful, and special fittings are available for this purpose. If the lights are to be used in a swimming-pool, they must be wall-fixed, as flex is dangerous to swimmers.

Installing lighting outdoors is usually a job for the professional, or at least for the gifted amateur, as there can be no make-shift-and-mend attitude about the choice of equipment and its maintenance. Outdoor sockets must be completely insulated against the weather, and armoured cable connections buried well into the ground (at least 460 mm or 18 ins). Cable has to be tough to resist the ravages of the elements and marauding pets, and any joins must be made by waterproof rubber connections. (Taping is never advisable.) Some garden lights operate from the mains voltage but are sufficiently well insulated to be used as they are. Others have a transformer which reduces the voltage to a safer level. The latter is a convenient system for do-it-yourself types, but if you are using any other form of mains voltage lighting in the garden, you must be absolutely sure that all exposed metal parts are earthed.

Hazards of a pathway at night are eliminated by a low-level toadstool-shaped lamp set in the greenery

Party lighting

Lighting for an evening party starts outside the house, for guests will feel all the more certain of an enjoyable evening ahead if they can see a welcoming light at your front door. There are, however, more practical considerations than this. For one thing, the number and/or name of your house should be clearly discernible from the road. For another, guests need to have their path well lit to the door. It is a bad start to a party if someone trips up the steps, ladders tights on a rose-bush or puts a foot in the lily-pond.

Once inside the house, lighting should match up to the occasion. It must be well thought out to set the guests at ease and to make the surroundings as agreeable and interesting as possible. The first – and last – point to consider is the hall. Even the most carefully-contrived party scheme, with controlled light and shade, interesting highlights and flattering glows, can be ruined if your guests have to say squinting hellos and good-byes in the penetrating horror of an overlit hall.

Most dinner-parties start and end in the living-room, with a long break in the middle for eating, either in a dining area or in a separate dining-room. Lighting in these areas or rooms should be complimentary. A dark and cavernous dining-room, lit by a few flickering candles, might create just the kind of setting you want for the meal, but walk out from there to the brilliance of an over-bright sitting-room for coffee, and you will find the atmosphere of your swinging party stultified in an instant. Human beings are very adaptable, but if candles are your idea of supper-party bliss, then make sure your guests will not be plunged into temporary blindness during the coffee exodus.

The sitting-room, used for pre-supper drinks, needs to be sufficiently light for everyone to see clearly who he or she is being introduced to. A name without a face doesn't mean much to anyone. Some interesting shadows offer a degree of protection for shy types, but none of these should be so intense that a guest who has unwittingly placed himself in its dark recesses feels isolated. Equally, your lighting scheme should not have pools of such brilliance that a visitor suddenly finds himself lit up like the main attraction, something he or she may not enjoy.

At the dining-table itself, candles are, of course, old favourites for dinner-parties and many people choose them not so much because they believe that candlelight is so flattering – it can produce some ghoulish shadows – but because of an association of ideas. For them, it represents the party spirit. Storm lanterns look decorative and reduce distorting flickers, but a well-planned system of electric lighting should be sufficiently adaptable to instil the festive atmosphere in a room without any need to resort to candles with attendant problems of cluttering up the table and possible fire risks, too. Lighting for the dining area is dealt with in the chapter on lighting around the house, page 15, so it is a question of experimenting to get the best results.

Outdoor parties

More and more barbecues are sold every year for al fresco entertainment, and it must be admitted that food cooked in the great outdoors, even if it is only a diminutive, town-house patio, does somehow taste better. If, then, you want to embark on a barbecue party, you will have to give a bit

A patio-party is illuminated by decorative star-shaped lanterns suspended among the branches of an ivy-clad tree. Interior light spills out through full-length windows

of thought to lighting. Some light comes from the barbecue itself, which exerts its own camp-fire charm but if it is a largish party where guests will wander or dance in the garden, additional lighting is essential.

First of all, light is needed to show up plates, knives and forks, food and drink set on a table near the barbecue. If you have small tables dotted around the garden, these too need a light of some kind, as do paths, steps and other outdoor hazards. In addition, lighting carefully placed amid trees and plants will add to the festive atmosphere.

Surprisingly little light is needed for an outdoor party and, in any case, to overdo things would miss the whole point. For the tables, candles in storm lanterns are practical as they do not require electric wiring, yet look decorative. For the rest of the garden, portable camping lights, fuelled by bottled gas or paraffin, are effective. However, if you have the sort of garden – and optimistic temperament – to cope with such parties as regular summer events, fixed lighting is the best answer.

For a Bonfire Night party some lighting is necessary as a safety precaution, to allow whoever is organising it to see clearly where the fireworks, matches and so on are. But do not have too many garden lights, as they will detract from the spectacle.

After-dark swimming parties are enjoyable on balmy summer evenings, but make sure that lighting lives up to the not inconsiderable accident risks posed by this sort of occasion. There's no need for arc lamps, but make sure your guests can see where they are going.

Children's parties

Children are usually at their worst at parties. Encouraged by numbers and allies, as well as by the fact that parents start off by being comparatively indulgent at such times, children can quickly ensure that the whole thing gets out of hand – at least as far as the best Ming-vase table lamp is concerned. Summer parties shouldn't need light, but winter parties do. It should be overhead, or wall-mounted, and comparatively bright. Do away with all table lamps and standard lamps; if things get rough, they will be the first to suffer.

A Christmas tree is an essential part of every child's year and is virtually obligatory for a Christmas gathering. Essential elements in its fairy-land decoration are miniature, coloured lights. These come in rows of 12 bulbs of different colours (usually 20-volt torch bulbs) or sometimes there are 20 on the string, in which case 12-volt bulbs are used. Those systems which have an even greater number – 70 or so – of the tiny Lilliput bulbs strung up together use 3·8-volt bulbs. It is important that all the bulbs on any one string are of the same voltage and that the total voltage of the bulbs does not exceed the mains voltage.

The worst part of Christmas tree lighting – as any patience-tried father will tell you – is finding expired bulbs. One failed bulb puts out the whole lot and it is a lengthy process going through, bulb by bulb, to find the culprit. The Lilliput bulbs are better in this respect, as failures do not affect the others. 'Flasher' bulbs which turn the whole set of lights on and off intermittently seem to have great appeal for children, but can be hypnotically annoying to adults. Some manufacturers include these bulbs in their sets; otherwise they can be bought separately.

Disco parties

If you want to go all out for a discotheque atmosphere, then real light-show techniques will do more than half the work for you. Pop music and linked lighting add up to the kind of groove that disco-goers like to find themselves in, however uncomfortable it may seem to parents and entrenched Mozart-lovers. The most sophisticated schemes involve linking the lighting effects to the sound effects. Very briefly, this is done by a special unit, filled with liquid crystals, which changes colour with the temperature. These changes in temperature (which are very slight) are brought about by tonal signals from a tape-recorder, record-player or even radio. The lighting reflects the music, even to the extent of analysing it into bass and treble with consequent changes of colour, intensity and pattern of light.

A simpler unit can be bought which is electrically operated quite independently of sound. It projects changing patterns of coloured light onto a wall or screen. These simple light-show units use low-voltage reflector lamps fitted with coloured wheels and can stand on a table or be fixed to a wall. Some people enjoy these light-show effects, with or without music, and find them so relaxing an antidote to the city hustle that they don't need a party as an excuse to set them up.

Ultra-violet lighting produces some amusing effects and is a simple means of transforming a humdrum room into an exciting background for a teenage party. This type of fluorescent light causes certain fabrics and finishes to glow in the dark. White nylon, for example, takes on a whole new, fluorescent dimension.

The tree-shaped dining-terrace is generally lighted at night by an overspill of interior lighting. Exterior lighting is in the form of a spherical wall lamp by the angle of two walls. Candles in ornate holders of varying height create a party atmosphere. Design by Robert Fisher and Rodney Friedman

Some technical data

The paradox of light is that we never see it; we see only objects that reflect it. So what is electric light, and why are some types of lighting different from others? The following notes will provide a guide, but if you are in any doubt about the technicalities of lighting, then check with manufacturers or with one of the specialist bodies.

Incandescent bulbs

The most common variety of electric light is the result of an electric current being passed through a tungsten filament, as seen in any ordinary light-bulb. The resistance the current encounters while flowing through the filament produces heat and when the filament becomes hot enough, it becomes incandescent and gives off light. An inert gas within the bulb increases the efficiency of the light by reducing the rate at which the filament evaporates.

Filament bulbs are available with a single coil of tungsten wire, or with a double coil or 'coiled coil', as it is called. The coiled coil bulb costs more but gives more light. All common filament bulbs have an average life-span of 1,000 hours. 'Long-life' bulbs which last for 2,000 hours are also available but they are more expensive. These are useful for light fittings which are difficult to reach, in which case you may feel that the advantage of infrequent replacement outweighs the disadvantage of higher price.

Filament bulbs should be bought to suit the voltage of the mains supply. If, for example, your house or flat is on 240 volts, buy bulbs of the same voltage. If your bulbs are designed for a lower voltage, their life will be reduced; if they are designed for a higher voltage, their light output will be reduced. The common sizes of domestic filament bulb range from 5 watts (for the dimmest of night-lights) to 200 watts, although the latter is seldom used and almost all household lighting needs are met by 40, 60, 100 and 150 watts. Remember, the greater the wattage, the greater the heat generated, so be sure that the shade is not too small, as this will lead to over-heating and consequent damage to both fitting and shade. If a particular wattage is recommended by the manufacturer of the light fitting, this advice should be followed.

The finish of the bulb plays a large part in its effectiveness for the job it is required to do. Clear bulbs create hard shadows and glare because the filament is fully exposed to view. These bulbs are usually acceptable for lighting a crystal chandelier using small candle-lamps, but even here glare can be a problem.

'Pearl' bulbs, which have a roughened finish inside the bulb, are slightly softer on their surroundings. Silica-coated bulbs, those with an inside coating of white powder, are kindest of all and give a soft, general light. These coated bulbs are preferable for most domestic light fittings.

Special shapes and sizes of filament bulbs are made for particular purposes. You can buy candle-lamps, for example, for some traditional fittings, or tubular designs for lighting a picture or display shelf. Coloured bulbs are also available for party lighting or other decorative effects. Mushroom-shaped bulbs are more compact than the usual pear-shaped ones and therefore may be more suitable for some shallow light fittings, but again beware of using too high a wattage just because the bulb will fit.

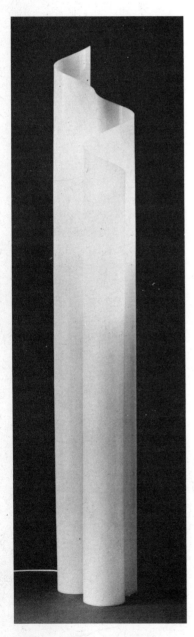

This curving sculptural floor lamp is designed by Vico Magistretti in white Plexiglass

Other filament bulbs

Other filament bulbs range from medical bulbs, the size of a pin-head, to monsters designed for television and film studios or lighthouse use, but of most interest to the domestic user are the reflector lamps which have a specially shaped bulb internally coated with silver or aluminium. This reflecting surface gives an accurately controlled beam which can be wide or narrow depending on the type of bulb. The cheapest versions are made of thin glass, are internally silvered, and are available in wattages of from 25 to 150. They have a soft edge beam and are used for many domestic spotlights. A more expensive version, made of thick toughened glass, is known as a pressed glass bulb. These are sometimes designated PAR bulbs and the 100 and 150 watt ratings are suitable for outdoor use, for lighting gardens or drives. They have a longer life, about 1,500 hours, and are more efficient than the internally silvered types. Inside the house, PAR bulbs are used mainly for cylinder downlighters and make for some interesting effects, although the heat generated can be a problem if used on a large scale. A special version known as a dichroic bulb is available which has less heat in its beam. This must be used only with a suitable fitting, as the heat in the direction of the bulb-holder is increased and may cause failure of the wiring.

A pear-shaped bulb with its 'crown' silvered is also available for use in conjunction with a special reflector fitting. This gives a very well controlled beam of light and can often be used to emphasise small items of display. Several special low-voltage bulbs are available; these are compact and have a variety of distributions but need a transformer.

Tungsten halogen bulbs are also sometimes used for domestic lighting. The light produced is very intense and efficient (having an output something like 15 per cent higher than the usual filament bulb) while the life of the bulb is actually doubled to 2,000 hours. These bulbs are sturdier and more compact, wattage for wattage, than the usual filament bulbs, and the 50 and 100 ratings translate well from their original use in projectors to use in low-wattage domestic spotlamps. Higher ratings, of 300w and above, are ideal for garden floodlighting.

Fluorescent lighting

Fluorescent tubes are very economical, as they produce something like four times as much light as filament bulbs for the same expenditure of electricity. In addition, fluorescent tubes far outlive filament bulbs, having a useful life of 5,000 hours for the up to 900-mm (3-ft) size and 7,500 hours for the 1200-mm (4-ft) size and above. Although, wattage for wattage, fluorescent tubes generate as much heat as filament bulbs, it is spread over a larger surface area and so the tube itself is at a lower temperature. This large area also results in shadows being very much softer.

Fluorescent tubes have no filament but rely upon an electric discharge taking place between two electrodes. This discharge generates invisible ultra-violet light which activates the powder on the inside of the tube causing it to fluoresce. By varying the composition of the fluorescent powder many different colours and effects can be obtained. Broadly speaking, two classes of fluorescent tube are available. The first, often

An arrangement of glass tubes with bubble ends forms this glittering chandelier

Silvered reflector lamps with soft, easily depressed bases for angling in any direction

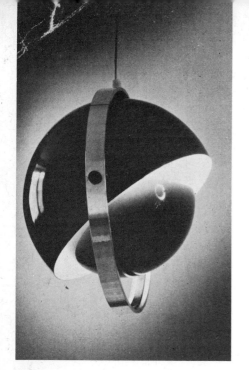

Egg-like pendant lamp in metal and aluminium can be easily rotated in all directions

known as the high efficiency tube, is designed to produce the maximum amount of light without consideration of colour rendering. The second class sacrifices some efficiency to improve the colour rendering of objects seen in its light. Within each of these two classes a range of colours is available from warm (pinkish) to cool (bluish). For domestic use, the tubes to avoid are the high efficiency 'white', 'warm-white', and 'daylight', although these may be of use in the attic or the garage. The tubes to be preferred for most living areas are the 'de luxe warm-white' types which have good colour rendering and an appearance that blends well with filament bulbs. While these are also suitable for the kitchen it is sometimes preferred to have a 'cooler' light, such as 'natural'.

Fluorescent tubes are available in a variety of sizes. They range from about 6 ins (150 mm) to a maximum of about 96 ins (2400 mm) with wattages spanning from 4 watts to 125 watts. Diameters vary, too, with the very low wattage tubes being $\frac{5}{8}$ in (15 mm) in diameter and the larger wattages at $1\frac{1}{2}$ ins (38 mm). An inbetween size measures approximately 1 in (25 mm) but this is available only in the 460-mm (18-in) 15w, 900-mm (36-in) 30w and the 1500-mm (5-ft) 50w ratings. Fluorescent tubes are also available shaped as circles, Us and Ws, in various shades of white. The straight tubes are available in a range of decorative colours.

The efficiency of a fluorescent tube falls slowly during its life and if the tube is 'black-ended', flickers, or has difficulty in starting, it should be replaced without waiting for it to give up entirely.

The commonest failings among fluorescent tubes used to be flickering and humming, both of which can develop into a torture-like situation for anyone particularly sensitive about these things. Both these problems can be controlled. Shielded-Cathode tubes, which reduce flickering, are now used and modern control gear is very quiet. It is possible, however, that if the fluorescent fitting is mounted on a reverberant surface this may act as a sounding-board and amplify the small sound. If this should happen, it is possible to remove the control gear from the fitting and position it elsewhere. This should be done only by a qualified electrician.

Bulb holders and fittings

The cap of the common filament bulb is usually of the bayonet type – that is, the 'push in and twist' type. Many of the spotlights, however, have a screw-cap and some of the smaller, special-effect lamps, such as the candle-shaped varieties, have either bayonet or screw-caps but of a reduced size. Tubular filament bulbs have a cap at both ends, usually a single contact peg and all modern fluorescent tubes have two bi-pin caps.

Many common filament bulb types are available with alternative caps, so check that you are buying a bulb with the right cap as well as the right finish and voltage.

Switching on light

Switches are something of a side-line when it comes to lighting yet, to anyone with an eye for detail, their appearance can often detract from the general setting.

For years, now, 'modern' switches have been made in off-white plastic which, presumably, was a colour that the manufacturers thought would go with everything, with the result that it went with nothing. Unless you are lighting an off-white room, the typical old-style switch looks a faded blotch, old before its time, on an otherwise pristine wall. Pure white is a better choice for most contemporary interiors as window-frames, skirtings and other woodwork are usually painted white, too. Fortunately, whiter-than-white switches are now being made, but don't expect an electrician or builder to install them automatically.

If the style of the interior is all chromed-steel and brushed-aluminium, silver-coloured light switches are more appropriate, especially if set flush into the wall for a streamlined finish.

The operation of switches also needs investigating. Some are based on the old 'flick' up-and-down principle. Others have a see-saw operation which is quieter and, although they are no revolutionary improvement on their predecessors, many designers feel they are more in keeping with the interior design of the 70s. Dimmer-switches have a circular knob which not only turns the light on and off but regulates its brightness. Some dimmers also incorporate an up-down switch, so that you do not have to select the setting you want every time you turn on the light.

If there is a series of lights in a room, it goes without saying that it is an advantage to have them wired up to separate switches, housed within the same back-plate. Table lamps, for example, can be operated by one, wall lights by a second, ceiling lights by a third.

Wall sockets for plugs are not as flexible, style-wise, as switches but, fortunately, they tend to be sited in less obvious places. Again, off-white plastic is the norm, although white-white versions are made if you look for them. A point to remember is that the plugs themselves are also made in both dead-white and off-white plastic. Whichever wall fitting you choose, make sure that the plugs are of the same colour. Flush-fitted, brushed-aluminium plug fittings look sleek.

If you are building a house or doing extensive alterations to an existing structure, look around carefully to choose the best sites for both wall switches and plug sockets. There is no need to stick to the conventional numbers and positions.

Two-way switches are useful in many places. In bedrooms, for instance, it is not just luxury but often a safety precaution to be able to switch off the main light from the bed as well as from the door. Garages with a door to the garden also need two-way switches – one by the main door and one by the rear door – so that you can drive in one way and walk out the other with no problem of how to switch off.

The usual height for light switches is not necessarily the right height for you. A tall family may prefer them to be sited slightly higher; a shorter family may find them more comfortable to use if they are set at a slightly lower level. In a child's room, it may even be preferable to have the switch lower still, to avoid grimy fingers stretching up the wall, inch by inch, until the tip-toeing feat is accomplished. Even better, though, is to install pull-cord switches which are absolutely safe and can be as long as necessary, becoming shorter as the child grows taller.

Bathroom lighting must be switched on from outside the room or by means of a pull-cord inside. This is to ensure that wet hands do not get the chance to come into contact with electricity.

Outdoor lamp, sturdily made to resist weather hazards, is both decorative and highly practical

Index

Numbers set in italics refer to the pictures